Hurricane Katrina Couldn't Break Us

Hurricane Katrina Couldn't Break Us

Edited by
Susanna K. Green

Sweet Nectar Publishing
http://www.sweetnectarpublishing.com

Hurricane Katrina Couldn't Break Us

Copyright © 2013 by Sweet Nectar Publishing

Edited by Susanna K. Green

Book Design by Wallace King

Supported by Sweet Nectar Publishing

PO BOX 48691, Tampa, Fl. 33646

All rights reserved. No part of this book may be reproduced, stored or transmitted by any means-whether auditory, graphic, mechanical or electronic-without written permission from the publisher, except in the case of brief excerpts used in critical articles and reviews. Unauthorized reproduction of any part of this work is illegal and is punishable by law.

ISBN 978-0-615-94075-5

Sweet Nectar Publishing

Remembering those who died; fighting for those that survived

*To those who suffered...
And are still suffering from the wrath of Hurricane Katrina
8 years later...*

You are not forgotten!!!

Table of Contents

Acknowledgements..................1
Introduction........................3

A frame in my Background
Robert Gibbons----------------------------------5

A Letter to Katrina
Mario D King-------------------------------------7

A Storm named "Katrina"
Willie Pearl Allen--------------------------------9

Hate the Home-Wrecker
Steven Boyd-------------------------------------11

Katrina
Randy Nino Robinson---------------------------13

Katrina Couldn't Break Our Spirit
Jasmine Lee-------------------------------------15

Katrina Couldn't Break Us
Darrell R. Freeman------------------------------17

Katrina's Rage, Saint's Survival
Justin Toney-------------------------------------19

Lift My Voice
Susanna K. Green-------------------------------21

Louisiana! A Beautiful Mold
Shani G. Dowdell-------------------------------23

Mississippi Didn't Miss Us
Nate Spears-------------------------------------25

Never Forget
Darlene Henderson-----------------------------27

New Orleans, My Home
Robert D. DoQui-------------------------------29

Promises
Alicia D'Amico----------------------------------31

Southern Phoenix
Angela James-----------------------------------33

Stronger Because of Her
Kitty Larue------------------------------------35

Tragedies of another Jerusalem
Latorial Faison--------------------------------37

Unbreakable Spirits
Quinton Veal----------------------------------39

We Are Free
Levi Mericle-----------------------------------41

We Made It
Martha Wilbon Green--------------------------43

Why Did I Leave?
Rev. Albert L. Green--------------------------45

A Letter from the Poets
Various authors-------------------------------47

Anointed Prayer for Katrina Survivors
Bishop J. Douglas Wiley Taylor...................49

Acknowledgements

Thank you... to all of the poets who permitted the use of their poems for this poetry anthology and for your kind, compassionate hearts that opened wide as you expressed your deepest well-wishes to encourage and bless another soul.

Wallace King, once again your talent has exceeded my expectations beyond measure; thank you for another outstanding book cover creation;

A special thank you to the former Mayor of New Orleans, Ray Nagin... for your endorsement;

Thanks so much to Iris B. Holton of the Florida Sentinel Bulletin for the splendid article and review;

I'm so thankful to my parents, Albert and Martha Green for their poetic contribution to this project... I love you both;

Bishop J Douglas Wiley Taylor... of Life Center Cathedral, much appreciation to you for your uplifting prayer and overall blessing upon this book;

Thank you to Louisiana native, Darrell Freeman, Jr. for inspiring the title of this book;

And, as always,
Thank you God...

Introduction

On August 23rd, at daybreak, Katrina formed over the Bahamas. Over the next six days it wreaked havoc in Florida, as a category 1 Hurricane; drifted out to the Gulf, strengthening as a category 3 and on August 29th, with wind speeds over 145 mph, hit landfall; leaving more than a million people throughout three states without power.

The states most affected by this devastating storm were Louisiana, Mississippi, Alabama and Florida, where hundreds of thousands of people were displaced from their homes and over eighteen hundred people were killed.

Between eighty and ninety percent of the residents of New Orleans were evacuated safely, in time before Katrina hit; although many remained in the city, mainly due to not having access to personal vehicles. The Superdome was used to house people that were unable to evacuate, but some residents opted to stay in their own homes and hope for the best. Eighty percent of New Orleans was flooded with some parts under fifteen feet of water that sat for at least three weeks.

People are still suffering physically and emotionally due to Hurricane Katrina with ailments such as anxiety, depression and PTSD.

Let's continue to pray for each other;

Prayer changes things.

A Frame in My Background

They said we would not make it
An experiment created
in the middle of a cypress swamp
A lone road from civilization
The bean-field spoke to me
As it did when I was a child
I could go there to be alone and dream
This is Zora's country; the dust-track
cannot be swept by broom
But it is as permanent as old
as grandma's syrup in big mason jars
She'd kept for years
until it caked around the corners of the lids
We would lick the frosting
From the caramel bowl
And they said we would not make it
The people of the muck
having to change with the season
Taking the clothes off the line
Before it was baptized in soot
The root of all things sugar
The plurality of who we are
And who we will become
Forgetting and not dismissing
not being ashamed of the gospel
of the lonely road
the crows of the rooster and the mills

The midnight sounds
and they said we would not be here
But this picture is a witness
Like grandmother telling us
we could go outside
She had one eye on us when she died
now the eye of the hurricane
They call us Isaac, Andrew and Katrina
They died of arthritis
and sugar diabetes, living and singing
Churches with one door to the altar
We called them saints
but it was our title and lives we were leading by
how can we say it's true
If we don't go back
get down and dirty and find the filthy in us
The musky back of an open cane truck
The love it takes
I remember this picture with all the hints
of paprika and cornbread crackling
Dead ancestors will have to answer to me and all
the generations that ate at the table;
This picture is the reason
This picture has its season.

Robert Gibbons

A Letter to Katrina

You came into our lives
On August 23, 2005
Your wrath started in the Bahamas
I sensed you coming as you approached my neighbor in the Gulf
Warnings from my mama—Nature
I watched you visit my cousins
Florida, Mississippi, Alabama and Louisiana
I could feel your heartbeat as you approached me
My children sought protection
You caused my insides to overflow
With your destruction, eruptions and disruptions
Who broke my levees?
Did I fail to mention you smell like corruption?
A large percentage of my body
Filled with your havoc
I cried…
During my pain, I felt neglected
Didn't receive assistance in time
Many died…
I watched, my children treated like savages
In the aftermath of what you created
Refugees are what they called them
Was their citizenship revoked or negated?
Racial tensions began to peak
Because of your deadly aspirations
Gone were the sounds of my children's horns
Dancing in the air
Gone was the laughter
Replaced with despair
Gone are the homes and buildings
My future children could inherit;
But what remained throughout it all
And continues eight years later…
Our Spirit!!!

Sincerely,
New Orleans

Mario D King

A Storm Named Katrina

Big city, bright lights
Tall buildings of various heights
The "Big Easy" New Or-leans
Great tourist attractions
And many pictorial scenes

In this big bustling city many lives were lost
When a storm name Katrina
Came roaring like a demanding boss

August twenty-nine two thousand and five
The winds blew and the waters came
The "Big Easy" was destined for change

Destruction, disaster of astronomical scope
Many left behind, clinging to hope
Those who listened and heeded instructions
Escaped the fury and ultimate destruction

Some had to experience the horror of it all
Spared by God to remember and re-call
Though it was a tragedy, a time of mental stress
Many eluded the worse
Others unconditionally blessed

But thankful to God I escaped without harm
Remember family and friends living far apart
Those who relocated undergoing a new start
Stamped in our memory
Like the Super Dome Arena
Is that historical storm
Known by the name "Katrina".

Willie Pearl Allen

Hate the Home-Wrecker

Remember when we use to play in the street
Not a worry, never hurried
Running fast with bare feet
Always a treat to meet
People coming and going
People smile all the while
Watching kids just growing and growing
Our house the happy home
Outside just kickin it
Street ball stickin and melted ice-cream
No worries just lick it!
So happy, me and my lil brother
Dad and mother so close
All in love
Could never be broken by another
But one day she came our way
Darkly dressed, wide hips
With a knock-down sway
Never seen solid structured men
Be reshaped like melted clay
We didn't know what to say
What were we to do?
Not used to this type of woman
That broke so many down
Everywhere she blew
And blowin…
I was crying as others were dying

So hard to believe
Thought the news was lying
We ran for cover just me and my brother
Dad at work and no sign of our mother
Amazed, we watched with big eyes
While water stank like tramps
Raised dresses over thighs
Then flooding our streets and hearts
Breaking up all the "death-do-us-parts"
Like those we made fun of
Living in shopping carts
We were now homeless
Our family broken apart
When the water dissipated
People we hated were elated
Nowhere to lay our weary head
Thoughts of mom and dad being dead
How would we be fed?
What would we do?
With no family close we had no clue
That was the day Katrina blew our way
And I'll despise her until my dying day!

Steven Boyd

Katrina

A tropical cyclone name Katrina
caused lost lives
The entire nation cried
The levee system catastrophically failed
What a horrible story to tell
All you heard was sirens and bells
Like the world coming to an end
Lord forgive us for our sins
Lost families, love ones, friends
Forced to start over, but where to begin?
Pure chaos and desperation
A terrible tragedy in our nation
People screaming, hollering, embracing
Slow to respond and time is wasting
My heart reaches out, it's aching
From the devastation New Orleans is facing
Where's the help when people need saving?
Much love to Mayor Ray Nagin
As the water rises, towers
The whole city lost its power
This unbelievable scene left me sour
George Bush is a dirty coward
Tears… pass me a tissue
Where's the aid from the governmental officials?
This should be their main issue
We now know the Government will diss you
Maybe it's because they were black
So let's take our time with that,
Let's wait around and lay back
They'd rather spend money to fight in Iraq
The may-lay caused by Katrina
Had citizens staying in the Superdome Arena
Plenty of sad faces and demeanors
America couldn't have been meaner
People dying, this is insane
U.S. Army Corps of Engineers
Is the first to blame?
What a damn shame
South Florida, Cuba, and the Bahamas

Mississippi and the Florida Panhandle
For them I light a candle
But New Orleans was destroyed, dismantled
The media classified them as "Refugees"
That statement offended me
What happened to equality?
Police officers pulling their weapons
Instead of assisting and helping
So senseless and I'm not accepting
To protect & serve is your profession
Helicopters above them hovering
People on roof-tops
The scene was troubling
This is my tribute to Katrina victims
Provided by "Sweet Nectar Publishing"!

Randy Nino Robinson

Katrina Couldn't Break Our Spirit

When people think of Mississippi
They think of slavery and farms
Well, I was born, bred
And lived amongst the corn
When hurricane Katrina came
I weathered the storm
Thanking God
It didn't cause me any harm

People came out
To help us repair the damage
But with or without help
We knew that we could manage
Hurricane Katrina
Couldn't break our spirit
Creeping through the night
Most of us didn't hear it

We rode around in the dead of night
Many with no water and very few with lights
We didn't sit around dwelling on how we felt
Instead we grabbed a beer
And fired up the grill.

Jasmine Marie Jones

Katrina Couldn't Break Us

We endured the rage of the storm
With a fierce punch, our lives changed forever
It destroyed our homes
Claiming the lives of many with terror

A lifetime of memories emerged
As tears poured down our faces
Trying to take more than our lives
Also our existence,
Everything we've worked for and built
Is now gone
Yet we still stand…
Katrina couldn't break us.

As the water rose,
So did our fear of death
But somehow we found the courage
To keep fighting and make it to the rooftop
As Katrina ripped thru the gulf coast
We continued to fight for our survival
The visualization of the devastation
Made everything surreal;

Katrina tore thru a lifetime of memories
As if it was useless debris
They labeled us refugees

Like an illegal immigrant sneaking across the border
What we went thru still troubles us today
Despite it all, we're still here, still standing…
Katrina couldn't break us.

God watched over us
Or we wouldn't be here
Katrina tried to take everything
But she couldn't take our heart
Katrina couldn't take our pride
We never lost our faith

The world embraced us with prayers
Hearts full of love
With a chance to start over
Katrina has made us stronger
At first, it seemed no one understood our struggle
Or our pain
As we stared death in the face
But we made it thru…
Katrina couldn't break us

Eight years later, we're still here, let's be clear
Katrina, the gulf coast is over you
You gave it your best shot, but guess what,
You still couldn't break us!

Darrell R Freeman Jr.

Katrina's Rage, Saints' Survival

Wards still wasted under water
Thousands of souls remain submerged
The stench of spoiled citizens stain the soil
She assaulted us without remorse

It's been 8 years since our
Refuge from her rage
Many still left homeless
Loved ones lost in the lakes of fire;

August 28, in Ward 8
Was the date and place
of my freak of nature fate
Peace and safety receded
as her winds clawed out communities

People snatched from their homes
Lungs suffocated by her hydro-blasts
That eroded contact between loved ones
Katrina would not stop roaring
As she painted the sky an evil ebony

It's been 8 years since our
Refuge from her rage
Many still left homeless,
Loved ones lost in the lakes of fire;

A mother struggled to save her son
He cried, "Mama, help me;
Please don't let go!"

"I won't let you leave me;
Baby, hold on!"
But as her last word escaped
Katrina snatched his soul
The mother's heart, levees broke
Screams thunderous as the storm
Katrina just abducted her only born
Like us, they missed evacuation
Left behind to drown in our sorrows
The nightmare of her nature
Became our worst fear
Her anguish claimed many Saints
As her latest tears

It's been 8 years since our
Refuge from her rage
Many still left homeless
Loved ones lost in the lakes of fire;

Many hearts not rejuvenated
But she couldn't snap our spirits
Though our structures collapsed
Katrina…
On rooted foundation
The Saints still stand.

Justin Toney

Lift My Voice

"*Help*," she shouted, tears welling in her eyes
"Can anybody hear me?"
A witness of her own demise
Cries rang out from despair
Gut-wrenching pain throughout the air
From the rooftops or overcrowded Superdome
Expressions of fear, marked numbers on homes

All too familiar of a poor man's plight
Just another time we had to fight
Water was scarce, food was without
Health declined from the awful drought
In need of medicine, to no avail
Relying on the system, not knowing it would fail
Bodies floated amuck, what a fright to see
Holding tightly to her bedrail
Praying "Lord, help me,"

Frantic, in a panic, screams in the air
Uncertain if this would be her last prayer
An array of emotions crowded her head
As she was determined to hold onto her bed
Wade in the water was just an old church hymn
Until Hurricane Katrina turned her hopes grim

Life as I knew it, just a distant memory
Heaven took its angels, who are now free
For those of us left, maintaining everyday
Given another chance by Gods sweet grace
Feeling grateful for all the lessons learned
Lifting my voice, leaving no stone unturned;

Hear me loud, hear me clear
I survived Katrina, I'm still here!!!

Susanna K. Green

Louisiana
...a Beautiful Mold

No matter how high
her tide rises
Nor the amount of treasure
her depth surmises
Insurmountable beauty brews within
From a speckle of dust
Blowing away with the wind
Slipping and sliding
Traveling to the lowest point
of the effusing bayou
Reacquainting the highest peak
To the lowest grove
Glowing and radiant
A sight to behold
Beautiful crescents
In the mold
Infallible…
Intangible…
Invincible…
A gift from God.

Angela James

Mississippi Didn't Miss Us

The Mississippi didn't miss us
We received no token of appreciation
When the pearly gates was ripping
Loudly leaking, loudly speaking
Help never reached me
All our burdens came to flood us
My death has come to blood
The reaper must greet me now
In this Bayou's mud;

I pray,
I pray my soul to take
With regretful sincerity
As side effects of Crawfish Etoufee
All things we've come to know
All things we've come to grow
All things we've raised up
Has flown on and now gone;

Diabetic issues,
Streets far from sweet
Hypertension hits the roof
Police guard the streets
Ordered to shoot
Anything that moves
Anything that breathes
This includes me;

I'm just a man
Trying to feed my family the best I can
Flood done flooded me out
My clothes, my street, the whole damn house
Wal-Mart's a disaster
Merchandise destroyed
I need a pair of boots
Please don't shoot me in front of my little boy;

He pulled the trigger anyway
But this can happen any day
I thought I was a citizen
More like a refugee killing

I was found black
He was found innocent
Not only during Katrina
Has this happened every evening
Prisoners left in cages
Reports with missing pages
Cheated out of promised wages;

All of this is evident
The Mississippi didn't miss us
The crowd around the Superdome
Paints the perfect picture.

Nate Spears

Never Forget

Who could forget about New Orleans?

Hurricane Katrina tried with all its might
To wipe New Orleans out of sight
It brought death, destruction and despair
Without a care, a nightmare
Like the ones you can't bare

Many people evacuated and got out of sight
Some just had to stay and pray every night
New Orleans could not withstand
The force from wind and rain
Nor the angry waters
That washed people away
But the culture's here to stay

When anyone thinks of New Orleans
They think food, music and more
New Orleans might not be the same city
But it is your city…

Who could forget about New Orleans?

Darlene Henderson

New Orleans, My Home

Her name like Poseidon's daughters evoke fear
Heartbreak, intrigue and passion
Her form was one of beauty
But as many now know
Beauty can be cold and heartless
She came wailing like a banshee
Her tears became the waves of destruction
That swallowed the city
New Orleans, my home
Her name, her very nature, is change
And change it did
She did…
We did…
KATRINA!
What once was, is now no more
Time to rebuild a better tomorrow.

Robert D. DoQui

Promises

The yellow dotted lines disappeared
As roads turned into ravenous rivers
And rooftops became floors
That housed frightened people
Drenched and wrapped in blankets
As they shivered;

One small five fingered little hand
Clenched on to her mother's shirt
The other, holding a tiny brown teddy bear
Tear stricken, pink cheeks
And swollen baby-blue eyes
As she looked to her father
For strength and prayer;

Surreal imagery surrounded them
In three hundred and sixty degree
Panoramic views
Fear and panic holding their minds hostage
As the rest of the world
Silently watched it unravel on the news;

Helicopters hovering above
Filming a tragedy too grave to comprehend
The little girl looks to the sky
And extends her arms
Waiting for a magical rope ladder to descend;

Eardrums drowned in confusion and despair
She faintly hears nearby neighbors yelling
"Help us, please!!"
But the helicopter turns around and leaves
Prompting desperate people to fall to their knees;

The little girl's father
Swallows back his own tears
Picks up his little girl and holds her tight
He looks at her, scared out of his own mind
But promises her that everything will be alright;

She blows out all sixteen candles
On her birthday cake
As she thinks of her wish, her heart beams
Every year has gotten better than the one before
And her nightmares have been replaced
By wonderful dreams;

She sees her mom and dad
In the corner of the room
And they are both consumed with laughter
This reminds her
That home isn't just a structure
But where her family is safe
Where there's promise for happily ever after.

Alicia D'Amico

Southern Phoenix

Eight years ago, your world forever changed
A wicked, unforgiving woman
Stormed into your lives
KATRINA was her name!

When she departed
Her anger, still felt and seen
Ravaged houses, water everywhere
Hundreds dead, nothing but despair;

After the shock, emptiness took control
Thousands left homeless, nowhere to go
Families separated, heartbroken and scared
Relief for some came too slow
How could this happen
In this Country of ours
Did the Government know?

She left her impact
For all the world to see
Showing all in her path
Just how "bad she could be!"

But like the roots
of your spicy foundation
You're Phoenix none the less
To the world and the nation!
You've come a long way since the Levees broke
The world said you were finished
Katrina was strong, but you are stronger
Your soul's fire couldn't be diminished!

Angela James

Stronger Because Of Her

Katrina at first stunned us all…
Government leaders, teachers and common folk
She moved faster than we could blink
But we improved because of her
Ripping through rooftops, windows and more
Teaching us with howling winds and rain
It's the power that she stirred within
Raising our voices, "Build again!"

Through heartache, loss and impossible woes
A wicked surge of air rose to a smarter state
A pride filled place,
Many said, "Let it go, just turn away,"
Through bitter tears and fears, begin again,
No more, if I coulda, shoulda, woulda,
Be Brave, be Strong!

Turn around; disregard the devastation in your path
See what must be held and grabbed
Grab your faith, build on that…
Grab your loved ones, friends, and fellow man,
Grab hands…unite and build again!

Katrina didn't bring us down
We are Stronger because of her!

Kitty Larue

Tragedies of another Jerusalem

With the fire of lightning
Ripping through ocean and sky
She came unsettling us
Leaving people without place
Alone, abandoned, erased
She was thrilling, a killing
A storm brewing without distilling
Filth and fatality from her flood
Drenched in despair
She came to claim us
We died and survived
This hell of high waters
With pens of scribes
We lift up our stories
Harmonies of our defeat
Tragedies of another Jerusalem.

Latorial Faison

Unbreakable Spirits

Katrina's destruction
Tore millions of hearts
apart around the world

The storm's behavior
opened my eyes
While watching its demise

Tears poured down my cheeks
Hopelessly
Each day passed without
the most basic needs

In the midst of tragedy
thousands lost their lives
In search of action
during that desperate time,
Yet unbreakable spirits endured.

I salute the survivors of Hurricane Katrina;
The heroes
You will never be forgotten.

Quinton Veal

We Are Free

You came as the sound of a hundred trains
Bearing prisoners at their plea

We yelled for you and screamed your name
"Katrina," please let us be.

We filled our lungs with rain and blood
With pain and a longing desire

No more homes where we rest our heads
Or warmth to place our fire;

Katrina, you took our hope and lives
It's because of you… we died,

You stole away what we've known and loved
But you couldn't steal our pride;

We healed our wounds, we buried our dead
We've felt the hate and sorrow

You may have defeated us today
But we'll build a new tomorrow;

Yes, you came as the sound of a hundred trains
But our tracks will forever be,

Planted in the land with a single phrase
"Katrina, we are free."

Levi Mericle

WE MADE IT

On that Sunday morning
August 28, 2005,
My nerves were bad
But I was still alive;

My husband wanted to stay
And weather the storm
But I was ready to pack
And leave him home alone;

He said, "We've been through this before
And nothing happened then,
When Katrina passes
Another will blow in."

He settled down to look at the news
What he heard changed his views
He looked at me with deep compassion
I knew then, it was time for action;

We left in hurry
Few clothes and little money
But I knew it would be alright
For me and my honey;

We traveled with our children to a friend
Confident that this would soon end;
We drove the highways and slept in our van
Met some good people that gave us a hand;

So now we are living in another city
Trying to make it our home
I'll never forget New Orleans
It's in my bones;

I miss my friends, the food
And all that's familiar to me
Spent a lot of time remembering
What use to be?

Yes, we went through the storm and rain
Had our heartaches and pain
Had our ups and downs
And thought no hope would be found;

Through it all, Hurricane Katrina could not break us,
We Made It...

Martha Wilbon Green

Why did I leave?

It wasn't that I didn't know it was coming
We could see it all over the news
The weather casters kept tracking the storm
But I kept ignoring their views
The city officials continued to warn everyone
But I like many others would not pack up and run
My house was strong and sturdy
Sitting high up off the ground
It had never flooded there before
Not since we had been around
We had lived there for twenty-three years
Through hurricanes and storms alike
It was not that I was so confident
Just hoping, I would be right
Katrina is coming! Katrina is coming!
Is what the reports would say
It's causing great destruction
And it's headed our way
Get out of the city! Get out of the city!
Mayor Nagin and others would say
They were getting my attention
More and more each day
My children were calling and asking
What are we going to do???
I didn't want to admit to them
That I truly wished I knew
I had not made up my mind
Even at that late date
But time was running out
And I couldn't continue to wait
I had been praying to the Lord
Please let this storm pass
But the will of the Lord must be done
Even though I had asked
The governor appeared on TV
And what she said horrified
Write your social security number on your body
To be identified
Now the hurricane was almost upon us
It was knocking at our door

With my indecision and procrastination
I couldn't wait anymore
It was now Sunday, August 28th
I looked to my wife and said,
"Honey, do you want to leave the city?"
She just lowered and bowed her head
She didn't utter a word
But tears were swelling in her eyes
That's when I knew
I was ready to say goodbye
We called our children and said,
"It's time for us to leave,"
I think this is the best decision
I truly do believe
So we met up at the church
On Dumaine and North Prieur
Where we prayed unto the Lord
To take away our fear
We got into our cars and began to drive away
Now you know why I left on that particular day.

Eld. Albert L. Green

A Letter from the Poets

There's nothing ordinary about tragedy, but it has a way of forcing us to explore deep inside our souls to rebuild and rediscover our truths.

Many lives unfortunately, were lost and families broken, just like the levees; but, what Hurricane Katrina tried her best to tear apart, while running amuck devouring everything standing in her way, she still couldn't break the true spirit within us.

Many saw horrific things that would normally only appear in a nightmare; which wasn't fair… but together, we will carry on as a nation of survivors who are stronger having endured insurmountable challenges and are still standing.

Our will to overcome this disaster has prevailed and our fire burns brighter than ever; a fire of hope to lamp the path on reconstructing the heart of home and love to overcome adversity with the help of God.

Anointed Prayer for Katrina Survivors

Our Father and Our God,

Our hearts are lifted to you in praise and thanksgiving. We bless, honor and glorify your great Name. We thank you that you alone are our refuge and strength, a present help in our time of trouble.

Through your mercy and power, you have kept our eyes from tears, our feet from stumbling and our life from death. You have brought us out of many waters and bore us on eagles' wings. In you we live, move and have our being.

O, Lord, we have burdened memories of the days of the storm. How fresh in our minds are the days when the ocean roared, the winds blew, and the rain fell. When the levies gave way, our city, our neighborhoods and our homes were destroyed. We remember when so many were swept into eternity; families were separated, many sought hope and help in other places, while a remnant of your children were left in horrible conditions, waiting for help that never came. But O God, we acknowledge that through it all, you alone were our strong tower, our hope and our help, our strength and our safe place.

We pray now for those now living in other places, while their hearts yearn for home. We lift before you the dispossessed and the disinherited, the needy and the neglected. Help us to know that all are precious in your sight. We pray for those hurting still, scared and bruised in places no one can see, but Lord God, You know! Be near to the lonely, the hurting and the broken; undergird those from whom all support is gone. We thank you that you alone have brought us thus far on our way and have given us courage for the living of these days.

We thank you for the reconstruction of our city and the rebuilding of our lives, thus far. Please forgive our sins and give us a heart of understanding of what you would have us to be and to do. Above all, may we seek to do your will as you grant us your strength and spirit? Send help and healing, grace and mercy to all that call on your name.

Now God, heal our yesterdays, strengthen us today and give us hope for tomorrow. Let your grace abound and your faithfulness sustain us. In you, we place our trust, in you we rest and in you we have peace. Bless your people here and everywhere and may we know that the long night is passing away and the joy of the morning has come.

We ask these things in the strong, mighty and victorious name of Jesus Christ, the Son of the living God; world without end. Amen. Amen and Amen.

Bishop J. Douglas Wiley Taylor
Life Center Cathedral

www.ingramcontent.com/pod-product-compliance
Lightning Source LLC
Chambersburg PA
CBHW071758040426
42446CB00012B/2613